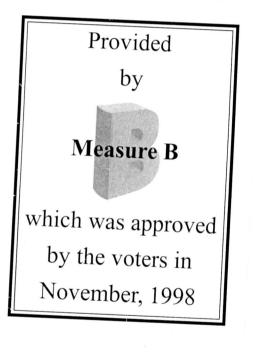

Provided

by

Measure B

which was approved

by the voters in

November, 1998

FROG

LIVING THINGS

FROG

Rebecca Stefoff

BENCHMARK BOOKS

MARSHALL CAVENDISH
NEW YORK

Benchmark Books
Marshall Cavendish Corporation
99 White Plains Road
Tarrytown, New York 10591

Illustrations by Jean Cassels

Library of Congress Cataloging-in-Publication Data
Stefoff, Rebecca, date
Frog / by Rebecca Stefoff.
p.   cm. — (Living things)
Includes bibliographical references and index.
Summary: Examines the physical characteristics and behavior of
frogs and presents many different kinds.
ISBN 0-7614-0414-7 (lib. bdg.)
1 Frogs—Juvenile literature. [1. Frogs.]
I.Title. II. Series: Stefoff, Rebecca   Living things.
QL668.E2S78 1997   597.8'9—dc21   96-39105   CIP   AC

Photo research by Ellen Barrett Dudley

Cover photo: *The National Audubon Society Collection, Photo Researchers, Inc.,*
John Mitchell

The photographs in this book are used by permission and through the courtesy of:
Peter Arnold, Inc.: Schafer & Hill, 2, 16 (bottom); Carl R. Sams II, 8 (top); Michael
J. Doolittle, 14-15; R. Andrew Odum, 16 (top); Ray Pfortner, 17; Hans Pfletschinger,
22 (left); R.M. Meadows, 23 (bottom); Michael Sewell, 32. *Animals Animals:* Joe
McDonald, 6-7; Michael Fogden, 8 (bottom), 12-13; John Netherton, 10-11; Zig
Leszczynski, 13, 20, 22-23, 23 (top), 24; Stephen Dalton, Oxford Scientific Films,
18. *The National Audubon Society Collection, Photo Researchers, Inc.:* Alvin E.
Staffan, 7; Karl H. Switak, 9; Gary Retherford, 10; Tom McHugh, 11; Tim Davis, 12;
Stephen Dalton, 19; Cosmos Blank, 21; Jeanne White, 25; S.L. & J.T. Collins, 26-27;
Nigel Cattlin, 27.

Printed in the United States of America

3   5   6   4   2

For Charlie

American bullfrog in duckweed, Pennsylvania

spring peeper

Have you ever heard frogs singing in the moonlight?

The deep, booming *baroom* of the bullfrog echoes across the pond. From the forest comes a high, buzzing *bree-bree-bree*, the call of the spring peeper.

bullfrog on lilypad

Frogs live
in all kinds
of places,
in parks
and ponds
and tropical
rain forests.

red-webbed tree frog, Costa Rica

See the big bullfrog squatting on the lily pad?
You might find a frog like this one in just about any
pond in North America. But you'd have to go to the
tropical rain forest to see the little green frog with
the red feet.

Some frogs live near ponds in dry parts of Africa.
In the summer, when the ponds dry up, the frogs
bury themselves in sand and go to sleep. They
won't crawl out of their burrows until the rains
come. Sometimes they wait a whole year for rain to
fall and wake them up.

green-and-black arrow frog

azure poison dart frog   *blue-legged strawberry arrow frog*

The bright colors of these frogs are signs that say "Keep away from me." These frogs are poisonous. They are called arrow or dart frogs. People in Central and South America dip their hunting arrows and darts in poison from the frogs. Just one tiny dart with frog poison on it will kill a large monkey or pig.

Argentine horned frog

crowned frog, Costa Rica

Some frogs may look funny to us, but there's a reason they look this way. The horns over the eyes of the Argentine horned frog help keep sand out of its eyes. The bumps on the crowned frog's head make it harder for a bird or a snake to grab the frog. And when the frog with the long flat nose goes swimming, it can stick its nose up out of the water to get a breath of air.

spatulate-nosed tree frog

large tree frog, Peru

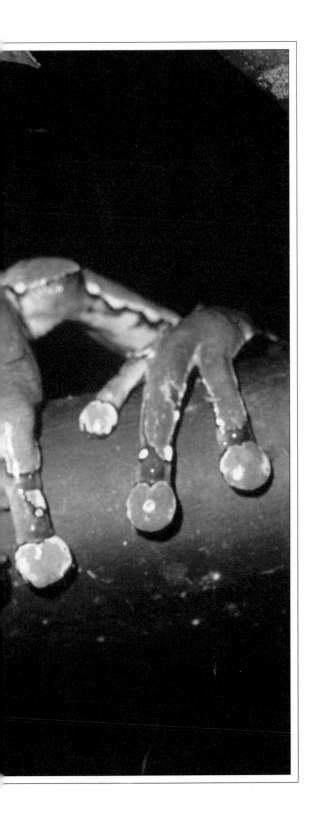

All frogs can climb a little bit, but tree frogs are very good climbers. They have long, bendable toes with round balls on the end of each toe. When a tree frog climbs up a tree or a wall, these balls flatten out and give the frog a tight grip.

Tree frogs roam the trunks and branches of trees, looking for spiders and insects to eat. They help keep forests healthy by eating caterpillars and beetles that harm trees.

Many tree frogs are colored gray, brown, or green to blend into tree trunks and leaves. Sometimes the frogs sleep under the leaves by day and come out after dark to catch night-flying bugs.

White's tree frog, also called dumpy tree frog, Australia

tree frog, Puerto Rico

In tropical rain forests, some tree frogs never come down out of the trees. They are born in pools of rainwater caught in flowers. This frog might spend most of its life inside one big flower.

leopard frog diving

leopard frog jumping

Frogs have long, strong back legs. They use these legs to dive and jump. You might be surprised to see how far a frog can jump. Measure a line five feet long on the floor. A big frog can jump this far. Can you?

bullfrog with ribbon snake

Frogs eat insects, worms, and other small animals—even other frogs. A hungry bullfrog may eat a small snake, but it will have a hard time getting the squirmy snake into its mouth!

Some frogs hunt for their food. Most frogs just sit and wait for something tasty to pass by. Then the frog jumps up, shoots out its long, sticky tongue, and pulls in its meal.

frog leaping at prey

All frogs are born in water. The mother lays hundreds of eggs in a thick, clear jelly. The eggs hatch into tiny swimmers called tadpoles. They have tails instead of legs. After swimming for a while, the tadpoles start growing tiny legs.

This tadpole is starting to look a lot like a frog, isn't it? Soon the little froglet is ready to leave the water.

four-week-old wood frog tadpole

Its legs are strong enough to jump and walk on land. It still has a small tail, but in a short while that tail will disappear, and the frog will be all grown up.

wood frog tadpole leaves water

Asiatic gliding frog

Summer nights are getting quieter. There aren't as many bullfrogs and spring peepers as there used to be. Frogs that live in forests and wetlands are losing their homes as people use more and more of the land. And because frogs spend part of their lives in water, they can get sick if the water is polluted.

young bullfrogs near a lily pad

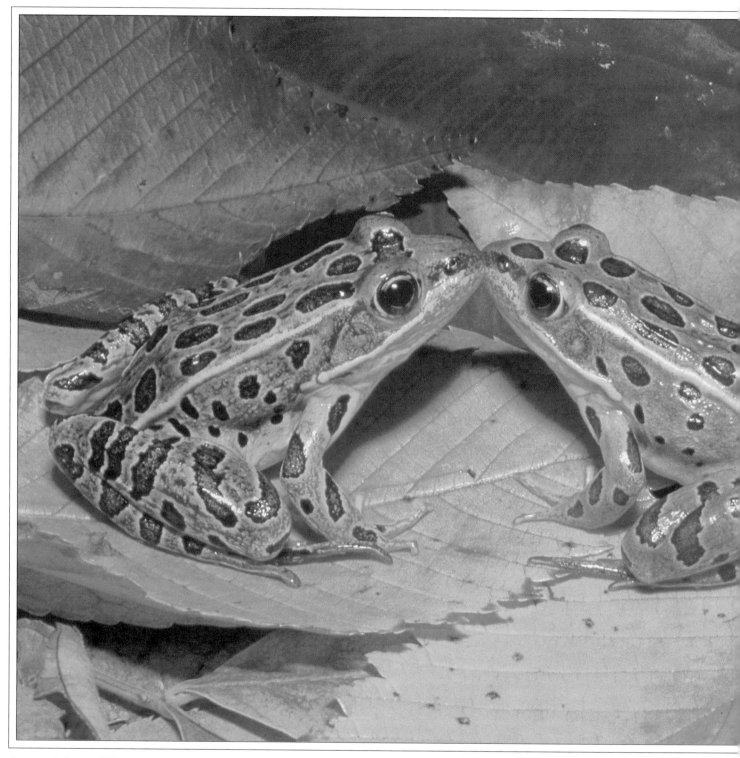

leopard frogs, Minnesota

green tree frog

Still, tadpoles wriggle in country ponds,
and bullfrogs boom in the summer darkness.
In tropical rain forests or in our own back
yards and parks, frogs hop and swim and
climb through the world of living things.

A QUICK LOOK AT THE FROG

Frogs are amphibians (am FIH bee ans). So are toads and salamanders. The name amphibian comes from Greek words meaning "double life." The amphibian's double life is lived in water and on land. Amphibians are born in water, but most of them spend part of their lives on land.

Frogs, tree frogs, and toads are closely related. They form a group of amphibians called anurans (a NYU rans). There are about 2,700 different species, or kinds, of anurans in the world. Here are five kinds of frogs, with their scientific names in Latin and a few key facts.

GOLDEN MANTELLA FROG
Mantella aurantiaca
[man TEH lah oh rahn tee AH cah]
A brightly colored frog found only in Madagascar, a large island off the east coast of southern Africa.

LEOPARD FROG
Rana pipiens   [RAH nah PEE pyens]
Found through North America from Labrador and Great Slave Lake in Canada south to California and Georgia. Once common in ponds, lakes, and roadside ditches throughout much of this range, now becoming rarer.

28

GREEN-AND-BLACK ARROW FROG

Dendrobates auratus

[den droh BAH tees oh RAH tus]

One of 135 kinds of Central and South American frogs that "sweat" powerful chemicals through their skin. More than fifty of these chemical mixtures are deadly to animals that try to eat the frogs. Scientists are using these chemicals to make new medicines for heart disease and other illnesses.

AFRICAN CLAWED FROG

Xenopus laevis   [ZEE noh pus LIE vis]

Sometimes called platanna. Has claws on feet for digging burrows in earth. Good swimmer, often found in or near lakes, streams, and ponds.

AMERICAN BULLFROG

Rana catesbiana [RAH nah cates bee AH nah]
Largest frog in North America. May be eight inches long (20 cm), not including legs. Lives in and around ponds and is a powerful swimmer. Can jump five feet or more.
Known for its loud, deep, booming call.

Taking Care of the Frog

Frogs that live in lakes, streams, and ponds need clean water. Tree frogs need trees. Many kinds of frogs are in trouble today because their habitats—the places they live—are disappearing. We need to save lakes, wetlands, woodlands, and rain forests so that the frogs of the world will always have a home. Some scientists also think that frogs in many parts of the world are becoming sick because of chemicals that we have put into the earth's air. The sick frogs may be warnings that we are making the atmosphere unhealthy for living things.

Find Out More

Clarke, Barry. *Amazing Frogs and Toads*. New York: Knopf, 1990.

Dallinger, Jane. *Frogs and Toads*. Minneapolis: Lerner, 1982.

Johnson, Sylvia A. *Tree Frogs*. Minneapolis: Lerner, 1986.

Linley, Mike. *Discovering Frogs and Toads*. New York: Bookwright Press, 1986.

Petty, Kate. *Frogs and Toads*. New York: Franklin Watts, 1985.

Index

Rebecca Stefoff has published many books for young readers. Science and environmental issues are among her favorite subjects. She lives in Oregon and enjoys observing the natural world while hiking, camping, and scuba diving.

northern leopard frogs, Minnesota